God's Christmas CARDS

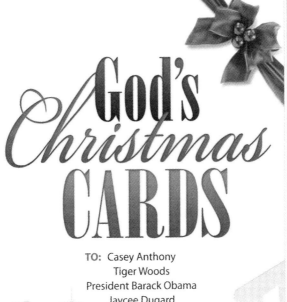

God's Christmas CARDS

TO: Casey Anthony
Tiger Woods
President Barack Obama
Jaycee Dugard
John Edwards
Bernie Madoff
YOU

Presented by

Dan Jackson *with* David B. Smith

Pacific Press® Publishing Association
Nampa, Idaho
Oshawa, Ontario, Canada
www.pacificpress.com

Cover design by Gerald Lee Monks
Inside design by Aaron Troia

Copyright © 2011 by Pacific Press® Publishing Association
Printed in the United States of America
All rights reserved

The authors assume full responsibility for the accuracy of all facts
and quotations as cited in this book.

Additional copies of this book are available by calling toll-free 1-800-
765-6955 or by visiting http://www.adventistbookcenter.com.

ISBN 13: 978-0-8163-2624-2
ISBN 10: 0-8163-2624-X

11 12 13 14 15 • 5 4 3 2 1

Contents

Introduction

It's a risky thing to be a ghostwriter or even a secretary for God! Paul underlines the difficulty when he pens in Romans 11:34: "For who hath known the mind of the Lord? or who hath been his counsellor?" There may be too many people today who are sure of what God thinks of them—especially in our nation's capitol—and are especially strident in their suggestions of what the Almighty thinks of their political foes.

Having conceded that point, we can still know with confidence what God would say to celebrities who have experienced spectacular moral falls. First, "be sure your sin will find you out" (Numbers 32:23). But then also, "where sin abounded, grace did much more abound" (Romans 5:20). And especially, "neither do I condemn thee: go, and sin no more" (John 8:11).

Even splashy sins like the adulterous sport-utility vehicle implosion of Tiger Woods or the failed sixty-five-billion-dollar Ponzi scam of Bernie Madoff are met with our Savior's tender mercies. No sin is so spectacular that it can't be canceled by the blood of the One Man whose sacrifice takes away the sins of the entire world. Especially this season, it seems, God has had to select many greeting card messages that offer both forgiveness and a new start.

After all, don't many secretaries do great jobs of sending out Christmas cards on behalf of their bosses? As long as they have a file of similar letters from past Decembers, the messages go out clearly. In these few pages of holiday cheer, we dip into God's past messages to some of His other children—as recorded in Scripture—to suggest messages He might send today.

Is it possible to know what God might write to a politician who gets involved with the wrong woman, gets her pregnant, tries to divert the press's clamoring attention over to an innocent aide, and then indignantly protests when confronted with the evidence? If we have any doubt at all of what the Lord's Christmas sermon to one John Edwards might be, we need look no further than 2 Samuel 11 and 12. Everything is right there except the postmark on the envelope and perhaps a gift certificate to the mall.

The recently departed Christian saint, John Stott, observed in his book *The Contemporary Christian:* "We could never have known [God] if he had not taken the initiative to make himself known." We can be thankful that God has sent an overflowing mailbag of Christmas cards to this sad and suffering world, and that we can glimpse His tender generosity by passing His letters around and taking them into our own hearts.

God's *Christmas* CARD TO
Casey Anthony

Dear Casey,

This is one of the hardest Christmas cards I've ever had to write. A card from God to Casey Anthony? It seems as unlikely as the whole universe turning upside down.

This is the magical, wondrous time of year when goodwill reigns and the whole Christian world is reflecting on an innocent little baby lying in a manger—My own Son. Fragile, helpless, vulnerable; needing His mom to be a good mom.

People sing carols about Jesus' mother. A young girl named Mary conceived her Child in pristine, untainted holiness, and then raised Him with stalwart affection and holy consistency. Baby Jesus had diabolical enemies, but His mommy was always there to defend Him—to stand watch over Him from cradle to cross. *"Can a mother forget the baby at her breast and have no compassion on the child she has borne?"* (Isaiah 49:15, NIV; emphasis added).

But what do I say to someone two thousand years later whose little girl goes missing for an agonizing month, while that someone enjoys the subsequent freedom of partying with her friends? The decaying corpse of your own child is wrapped in a Winnie the Pooh blanket, stuffed inside a trash bag, while you take a trip off to a tattoo parlor, seemingly cheerful and at ease, paying Bobby Williams sixty-five dollars to decorate your arm with an intricate design of *Bella Vita*. Your little girl is dead, and you think you now have a "beautiful life"?

There are some things that, for a season, are hidden from the world's eyes. Many young girls know the miracle feeling of discovering there's a tiny life growing inside of them. And maybe for a few days or even weeks, no one else knows. Then a doctor. A husband. Parents. Friends. The Facebook network. But for a little while—*shhhh*—it's a beautiful secret.

The reality, of course, is that I know right away. Heaven smiles; the angels celebrate. We all look forward to treasuring and guarding that tiny life. My Son and I mark out a spot up here where that new being created in My image will perhaps claim a mansion for eternity. So the very moment that Caylee Marie Anthony was conceived, I knew it had happened. I'm saddened by the reality that many of My children ignore Heaven's proven blueprint for a thriving family: you weren't married to Caylee's biological father, and, to this day, that bit of paternal information hasn't been registered in any earthly court. But I don't hold unborn babies responsible for the shallow carelessness of their parents, and I had a delighted hand in shaping the DNA and the fingers and toes and beating heart of your little Caylee. I was there, I was aware, and I was greatly in love with her that Christmas before she was born.

Then there was another thirty-one-day stretch where you had this treacherous, dark secret in your heart. What had happened to your little three-year-old? Where was she? You'd left your parents, George and Cindy, and gone zipping off to Orlando. You had an awesome job at Universal Studios, you boasted. Not true. When Grandma asked to speak to Caylee, you always said, "Well, not now, she's at the beach." Not true. Or that you had a really great new nanny for Caylee, a woman named Zenaida "Zanny" Fernandez-Gonzalez. Definitely not true. And when this murder case finally went to trial, there had been so many prevarications that the prosecution and defense teams had to combine to call 106 different witnesses! You twisted the truth so much that it took twelve days just to import a change-of-venue jury and impanel them.

Casey, you've spent most of your entire life spinning falsehoods. You know that, and you know that I know that. The police spent arduous months looking for Caylee's disintegrating corpse, when all along, you knew she wasn't missing. A search group is now suing you for one hundred thousand dollars, since that's what they spent looking for your little girl in all the wrong places. We all heard the psychologist's comment after the global uproar when you were acquitted, " 'They've been whipped up into a lynch mob.' . . . Nobody likes a liar, and [Casey] Anthony was an habitual liar."

But here's the honest reality about the methodical spinning of planet Earth on its axis every twenty-four hours: I see—everything—every moment, every detail, every deed, and every thought. It's not hard for Me; I don't have to focus or concentrate or shut out someone else's pain or rebellion in order to record yours. It's just that I'm God. I have seen every moment of your life, in full view, fully lit, impeccably documented and logged for eternity, including all the events that transpired on June 16, 2008. So even though the prosecutor wasn't able to produce any hidden-camera footage or successfully nail down the precise time line of what happened by the family swimming pool, what happened in the trunk of your white Pontiac Sunbird, or how a tiny female skull with duct tape on it came to be out in the woods, you can know that I know. But even before the medical examiner began to painstakingly reassemble the disintegrating skeletal bits recovered by police, I had the full story, with no gaps in the chronology. The trial transcript may surpass the fifty thousand pages that it took to record the O. J. Simpson saga, but I don't have to commission anyone to write down or time-stamp what I know about your case, Casey. I simply know.

I like how one of My most devout disciples, A. W. Tozer, described what it means to be God and have this divine attribute of omniscience. Here's what he writes, "God knows instantly and effortlessly all matter and all matters, all mind and every mind, all spirit and all spirits, all being and every being, all creaturehood and all creatures [including your little girl], every plurality and all pluralities, all law and every law, all relations, *all causes, all thoughts, all mysteries,* all enigmas, all feeling, all desires, *every unuttered secret,* all thrones and dominions, all personalities, all things visible *and invisible* in heaven and in earth, motion, space, time, life, death, good, evil, heaven, and hell."

As he goes on to say, I don't learn things. I heard what the jury heard, but I didn't learn a single new fact during those six weeks. I already knew. I heard forensic evidence about DNA and that rare brand of duct tape. I already knew all that. Someone at your house seemed to have gone online and looked up the word *chloroform*. You said it wasn't you. Your mom, Cindy, stepped forward to say that, oh, she must have done it. You said that your father had sexually abused you. He said he didn't. And on and on it went for six weeks of head-spinning contradictions and perjured testimony, during which I, God, sat watching with an aching, loving heart, learning absolutely nothing I hadn't known from the very first moment. In the judicial system, they call parts of the legal process "discovery," but that word means absolutely nothing here in the heavenly courts.

And after two days of human jury deliberation, "discovery" wasn't enough. With the so-called CSI effect going on in the courtroom, people assumed that the DNA and the fingerprints would be enough. But they weren't. "Use your common sense," said the prosecutor as he vainly tried to persuade the jury to convict you. "No one makes an accident look like murder." Members of the jury later stepped before cameras and admitted that they were dying to convict you. Every fiber of their being wanted to slap a death sentence on you and put in the needle themselves. "But it wasn't there"—meaning the evidence. One jurist said, "Everybody agreed if we were going fully on feelings or emotions, . . . she was done. I just swear to God. . . . I wish we had more evidence to put her away. I truly do. *But it wasn't there.*"

It was here instead. I'm the only One who knows.

Isaiah once wrote in chapter 40:13, 14, *"Who has understood the mind of the LORD, or instructed him as his counselor? Whom did the LORD consult to enlighten him?"* (NIV; emphasis added). In *The Message* paraphrase: "Who could ever have told God what to do or taught him his business? What expert would he have gone to for advice, *what school would he attend to learn justice?*" (emphasis added).

In a way, Casey, this is a message that transcends My Christmas card just to you. The rest of the world out there thinks it knows everything. No; but I do. Your trial exploded into a global circus, one of the most watched legal events in history. Every talk show wanted your parents, the judge, the jury, and the witnesses. There was a news explosion and millions of people dropped everything to watch. They sent more than ten Facebook posts per second with their reactions. And people were outraged because they were sure they knew more than the jury. They protested and picketed and burned up their blogs because they figured you'd gotten away with murder. But the fact remains that I know. The buck always stops here. Justice may be delayed but never denied. People may escape a Florida death sentence, but then they still meet Me.

Is that terrible news—that I know all things? You've done some terrible things in your life; does it overwhelm you that not one moment has been hidden from My unflinching gaze?

Let Me tell you something about My twenty-twenty vision, Casey. It's a warm and healing blanket encircling My universe. I see all things with the eyes and the heart of a loving Father. I weep for people's mistakes, but I don't hate the people. I see sins; I hear lies; I witness murders. And I want to reach out and touch, to restore and recover, to comfort and heal. My omniscience isn't a sinister thing, an Orwellian "Big Brother" computer network, or a spying satellite camera. In her classic good-news book, *The Unselfishness of God,* My child Hannah Whitall Smith tells about a friend who grew up with a childish sense of chilling terror, because she figured out that God saw all things. She had this dreaded vision of a kind of heavenly Cyclops, a one-eyed, angry deity in the skies, who spied on her with this single malevolent, unblinking eye, writing down her little flubs and sins and wanting to blast her right into hell.

Finally, her mother figured out what kind of visual torment this child had been experiencing all these weeks. "No, no, no," she said soothingly. "Sweetie, no!" She explained that I am a Friend, just like My Son, Jesus. Yes, I see all things—but with eyes of love, eyes that weep in sympathy, eyes that hope for good and mist over with the hurts and sorrows of life. Just like King David, who once wrote with amazing gratitude in Psalm 139:7, *"Whither shall I go from thy spirit? or whither shall I flee from thy presence?"* (emphasis added). Not wanting to, not desperate to get away from Me, but simply acknowledging the wonderful reality that I am always with My children. Even the most desperate sinner might scuba dive down to the deepest part of the ocean, David says, but I'd be there waiting for him or her with some extra oxygen. And so Hannah Whitall Smith, remembering her friend's earlier misconception, confessed in the end: "And when she went to bed that night she fairly laughed out loud at the thought that such a dear kind Eye was watching over her and taking care of her."

In a moment, I have two Christmas messages for you, Casey, beyond the obvious one, which is this: I love you. I honestly and truly love you here at Christmastime 2011. Much of the world hates you; I don't. They want nothing to do with you, but I still want to have everything to do with you. The prosecutors may refer to you as a girl with "imperceptible moral character," but I see the good in you. A lot of people are no longer willing to be your friend, but I'd like to be your best Friend. When you were sentenced to only four years in prison, with time already served counting against that, and then were released this past July 17, you became a global pariah. You're so isolated now, so alone and shunned by society that you have to take college classes online. Not very many people want to come anywhere near a twenty-five-year-old girl who they all assume killed her own daughter. But I love you and would be proud to claim you as My child if you want Me.

But now the two tough messages. You could be set free, not in terms of the judicial system, where what they now call freedom is to you a hollow joke and nightmare. You're more in prison now than if Judge Perry had sent you to death row. The judge ruled your many false statements as just four misdemeanor counts, but you know full well how your empty life of falsehoods mocks you now. As My child Brock Clarke once observed, "Sometimes the lies you tell are less frightening than the loneliness you might feel if you stopped telling them." But there is a hill called Calvary, there is a doctrine called grace, and there is such a thing as forgiveness and restoration. I can adopt you as My child, and I can give you eternal life. I can even reunite you with Caylee. Because your little girl was never lost from Me—not for the least moment. She has been "Safe in the Arms of Jesus," and I can make everything perfect, better than before.

But first you have to accept this about Me: I love you and I know. There can be no more lies. No more inventing of fictitious nannies. No more trying to exclude DNA. Confession and forgiveness and salvation begin with—confession. I already know what happened that day. I know what happened to Caylee. And I'm perfectly willing, even eager, to have you come right to Me and fall into My arms and be eternally loved. But it would have to begin with you stepping away from your defense and appeals to the Fifth Amendment. The truth and the cross of Jesus would have to be your only defense; I really don't ever pay attention to anything else.

The second message I have reaches out to you and also to millions around the world who were breathlessly glued to this trial, who asked, "God, where were You when all of this happened? An innocent little girl was unfairly deprived of life. What happened? Aren't You God? If You know all things, can't You also *do* all things? Can't You prevent evil? You allowed justice to be stood on its head here."

Casey, very few people know exactly what you did; but you know and I know. Could I have lifted My hand and prevented Caylee's death? Yes, I could have. You know what it would have taken, but I could have stepped in.

I could have stopped Hitler. I didn't. I could have stopped Osama bin Laden. I didn't. I could have stopped you in your tracks, not just with Caylee, but many, many times when you were about to lurch into danger or something that would be destructive to yourself and others.

But the only way I could be that kind of all-powerful and all-intervening God would be if I were to guide *and guard*—and manipulate—all aspects of your life. To coerce your obedience. In other words, I would have had to create you as a robotic slave, a compliant but unfeeling subject. Yes, I could have programmed you to only do good. But if I shape a mother who has the glory of free will, the ability to love or to ignore, to protect or to kill, she then does possess the awful freedom to sin and rebel, to make heart-shredding and scarring choices.

This is why there was a 9/11. This is why the O. J. Simpson trial, and now your sordid story, were permitted to unfold in agonizing and sketchy half-truths. I could have stepped in front of Eve before she reached out and picked that fruit. I could have grabbed her wrist and stopped the whole war right there; it would have been easy for Me to just kill the snake, as people say, and be done with it. But Adam and Eve had free will, and so do you.

There's coming a day—and this is hard to explain, even for God—when Heaven will fully triumph. Courthouses and cemeteries will be distant memories. The prisons will be emptied; little girls and their moms will be reunited. And in that better land, people will still have free wills. They won't be robots there either. I've never much cared to be surrounded by digital worshipers, and I have no plans for that. But when the new earth is launched, and it carries forward for the next ten thousand years and beyond, it'll be a place populated by citizens who are loyal to the Christ child. They could choose to rebel—*but they won't.* They'll still have hearts that love and minds that think and weigh, but they will all choose loyalty and worship. With Calvary forever in their hearts, it will be their highest joy to be loyal and to worship.

That was My dream kingdom for Eden, and it's what I want to personally offer you, My child, Casey Anthony, as My special Christmas gift for 2011.

I love you!
God

God's *Christmas* CARD TO
Tiger Woods

Dear Tiger,

This is My busy time of year, so I know that eavesdropping holiday shoppers will understand that God's message to you is three things. First, yes, it's My Christmas card for you here in 2011. I know you have a Buddhist background and heritage, and I'll say a few words about that in a moment. But I wish you and your loved ones a "Merry Christmas."

Second, is it all right for Me to wish you a happy birthday here as well? Plenty of sports fans mark your birthday as coming just five days after a lot of people celebrate My own Son's birth down in Bethlehem. So happy thirty-sixth birthday, Tiger. People say that next year has got to be better for you—there's nowhere to go but up—and I certainly hope it is.

But third, I have to admit that this is an unabashed fan letter. I love you—and I love watching you play golf. There aren't many things more thrilling than to see you hit a smoking long drive straight down the middle of a lush fairway at the U.S. Open. Or to watch in anticipation while you chip out of a monster bunker at St. Andrews to save par, or sink a forty-foot eagle putt at the Masters Tournament. You've got that Nike golf cap and your trademark red shirt—yes, we know, "aggression and assertiveness"—that you traditionally wear for the final Sunday round as you close in on another of your seventy-plus Professional Golfers' Association (PGA) victories with a fist pump on the eighteenth green. You made golf fun to watch, and whenever you were away from the game, almost half of the TV audience would go find something else to do.

I've always said to My favorite people, "I knew you in the womb." And, of course, you almost had a putter in there with you. You were playing golf by the time you turned two. I saw you out-putt Bob Hope on *The Mike Douglas Show* when you were two! Showing up in *Golf Digest* at the age of five was almost as impressive as shooting a score of eighty as an eight-year-old and going on to shatter every high school record on the books there in Anaheim.

I love that story floating around from your college days when a couple of your dorm pals bragged about getting tickets to some big sporting event. And you came back with, "Well, I'm gonna go to the Masters." "Wow," your friends said. "You must know somebody. How'd you get a ticket to that?" And you just looked at them. "Dude—I'm *playing* in it."

You came in forty-first, but when you quit college to turn pro, you began to win, and win, and win some more. Before long, other players began to settle into a feeling of, "well, we're all competing for second place, because Tiger's got the trophy pretty much sewn up." Whenever you were in a tournament, the other golfers swung so hard—overcompensating—that your mere presence statistically added a full stroke per round to everyone else's score. Major courses around the country had to start adding extra yards to all the holes—"Tiger-Proofing," they called it—just to try to slow you down a bit.

What turned the world of sports upside down in 2009 was that all of your fans who knew only the good about you, suddenly learned the bad as well. Like the sudden crash of an SUV, your carefully nurtured public image was abruptly shattered. And the hard thing for Me, Tiger, was to know both sides all along. Every day, every golf season, I had to endure seeing the ongoing hypocrisy, the two sides of the same coin. To witness the dark along with the carefully crafted light, the selfishness along with the charity events, the illicit rendezvous that ran parallel with the much-heralded wedding to your beautiful bride Elin.

You had a work ethic that was the model of the world of golf: no one trained like you did. No one else had the discipline. No one else honed their craft with as much single-minded purpose. And that's all the golf world knew. It was wonderful. You had taken the entire sport to a new level, and people rightly sang your praises for that—but the flip side was that you quietly said to yourself, over and over, "Now I'm entitled to do whatever I want. I deserve extra moments of pleasure, extra samples of the forbidden fruit. I'm Tiger Woods. All the rules for everybody else, they don't apply to me. I can sleep around in Vegas and the press will cut me some slack because I'm Tiger Woods."

You set up the Tiger Woods Foundation and helped children all around the world. You gave out university scholarships. Your advisors helped you set up Start Something, a program to help kids develop character, as ironic as that seemed to Me. You did free golf clinics all around the world—and there were always TV cameras recording the good deeds. You got Sting and Bon Jovi and Stevie Wonder to perform at various Tiger Jams, which have raised ten million dollars for charity.

And then, when the camera crews went home, you had a one-night stand with the neighbors' daughter. You could afford to have porn stars fly here and there to meet you at various tournaments. You had to quickly agree to appear on the cover of a fitness magazine as a quid pro quo backroom deal to get a tawdry gossip newspaper to squelch a story about your affair with a waitress.

Of course, when you finally ran your Cadillac Escalade into a hedge, then a fire hydrant, and then a tree, well, then, everyone knew. Most of the planet's citizens, whether they watched ESPN or not, were quickly aware that one Eldrick "Tiger" Woods was a womanizing cheat, a scoundrel not worthy of the gentleman's game of golf.

And so here we are, Tiger. And again, this is fan mail. Listen to Me, world: I love Tiger Woods! I really do—as a golfer and as a human being. But Tiger, here's My Christmas question, Who are you? Really? And who—or what—do you want to be while going forward? Because I have a Christmas gift for you.

You came up with a great word: *Cablinasian.* "That's what I am," you told reporters. One-quarter Chinese, one-quarter Thai, one-quarter African American, one-eighth Native American, one-eighth Dutch. So *Cablinasian* was a fast way of abbreviating Caucasian, Black, American Indian, and Asian. Is that what you are?

For thirty-six years, you've been defined by certain other things, too, and they've all turned out to be fragile and fleeting. You were perennially the world's greatest golfer, holding the number one ranking. That was Tiger Woods's global label: you always, always won. Well, no more. This year you were forced to skip the U.S. and British Opens. One year ago, you were still ranked number one in the world—now you're not even ranked in the top fifty.

Do you wish for money and wealth and excess to be your defining label? Your skills and your marketing reputation created a billion-dollar stash of cash. It was enough to let you buy a thirty-nine-million-dollar property in Jupiter Island, Florida. But the $164 fine you had to pay when you plowed into that tree at two-thirty in the morning, that was just the beginning of your glittery empire seeping away. When the sleazy stories began to scream their way onto the Internet, the endorsement deals went away.

Oh, you'll always have plenty of money, even with your multimillion-dollar divorce settlement and what you have to pay in child support for Sam Alexis and Charlie. But any person whose identity—whose inner defining characteristic—is based on money runs the turbulent risk of losing most or all of that cash, and experiencing the hollow understanding that *celebrity* due to having a lot of money truly doesn't say very much about a person.

King Solomon was a man who had more money and more girlfriends than even you could ever comprehend, and he finally looked back and cried out in sorrow, "Dear God, what have I got here? Nothing but vanity. It's worthless 'cause I'm lonely and miserably unhappy. It's like chasing after the wind."

I became good friends once with a man named Jack, who passed to his rest before you were born. He was brilliant; he wrote books; he had admirers; and he filled up his life with the shallow pleasures of being admired and of besting his friends in wordplay while sipping a pint of beer in a Cambridge pub. He carefully crafted this identity that was admirable in a secular way with his PhD degree, his book royalties, and the people he bested with his wit and his sarcasm.

And then one day, he looked in the mirror and saw how horribly empty and vapid and tawdry it all was; trophies and fame but no joy. As he journeyed from atheism to being a believer, it was wrenching to let go of all his former emotional props and crutches. But then in his bestseller *Mere Christianity,* Jack, whose real name was C. S. Lewis, wrote with sheer relief at how good it was to be humble, "delightedly humble, feeling the infinite relief of having for once got rid of all the silly nonsense about your own dignity which has made you restless and unhappy all your life." And, of course, the irony is that as a Christian writer who embraced being My child and My follower, he experienced more fame and royalties and headlines than ever before. Only now, he knew what to do with the glory; he passed it right on to heaven and just stayed on his knees a bit longer.

Tiger, please let Me say two things to you—again, as a Friend. You have been a man who demonstrates excellence in your craft. More Christians desperately need to strive for excellence the way you always have. The world of sports will never be the same because you trained so hard and set an example of diligent, persevering hard work. The kingdom of heaven doesn't begrudge successful people the fruits of their labor. Headlines and interviews and dignified celebrity and the appreciation of fans can all be healthy realities in the world of sports or any other endeavor.

But does a man put the things of God first? Does your first identity come from your swing and your trophies and your endorsements and your money? Or does it come from the fact that you're My child and that you put Heaven first and that you are seeking first the kingdom of God and His righteousness? Jesus had twelve disciples who were always clamoring for the number one seed, so to speak. And He finally said to them, "The important thing is to be My friend and have Me be yours. That's it."

In Luke 12, Jesus tells a little parable about the Tiger of His day, a man who made so much money as a gentleman farmer that he allowed his agricultural successes to be *his* defining characteristic. "I've worked hard; now I'll live the good life," he said to himself. "I deserve these extra things because my name is—Nehemiah Woods." Or whatever. And as My Son tells the story, the man died that very same night. Who got all the money and the overflowing barns then? But more important, that man was a fool because he didn't put eternal things first.

Tiger, I would love to see you become number one in golf again, as long as golf becomes number two to you, right after your friendship with Me. It was tough for you in 2006 when your dad and mentor, Earl Woods, died. But if you truly let Me be your heavenly Father—let Me love you and lead you and take care of you—then things will be all right. Everything else in your tumultuous life will fall into place.

Here's the second thing. You had said in your mea culpa press conference that you had strayed from the Buddhist faith of your childhood. Which is tragically true. I have millions of dear children of Mine, faithful, wonderful people—men, women, and children—who, often for good and understandable reasons, are adherents of the Buddhist religion. I follow their lives with deep interest and love them with intensity.

And when they follow that heritage with sincere diligence, it makes them humble and cheerful and pure. It leads them to put others first, to deny self, and to care for the suffering world around them. There's no denying that your life would have been much more productive if the Buddhist faith of your mom had found a more substantial place in your high-flying life. You once admitted, " 'Buddhism teaches me to stop following every impulse and to learn restraint.' " Then, looking back over the carnage of your irresponsible acts, you added sadly, " 'Obviously I lost track of what I was taught.' "

If there's any athlete in America with the steely determination, with the self-discipline to turn over a new leaf and make a fresh start, it would have to be you, Tiger Woods. But healing doesn't simply come from saying, "Now I change courses. Now I try harder. I look within and remake myself as a new man. Now I walk on this different road." No, it also involves seeking forgiveness for the mess. You are a man who has sinned grievously, Tiger. Money can't pay back what you stole. You can't buy off all of these mistakes. A thousand reincarnated lifetimes of hard work and good golf can't undo and erase the scars. You need forgiveness and you need the record expunged *and you need a Savior.*

Here during the Christmas season, you need what the Christ child came to your hurting world to offer the Christians and the Buddhists and the atheists and—well, everybody. *For unto* us—everybody, the whole human race—*for unto* us *a Child is born. Unto* us *a Son is given* (see Isaiah 9:6).

Tiger, may I offer you a Christmas gift? It can be yours right now with no blisters or qualifying preliminary rounds. You don't have to make the cut. And it can be yours forever. It's the robe of perfect righteousness, of amazing grace salvation, offered for free to you and all citizens of planet Earth. It's rather expensive, actually. My Son and I went shopping and paid quite a dear price for it, to tell you the honest truth. But I'd really like for you to have one.

Merry Christmas, Tiger.

Love,
God

God's *Christmas* CARD TO
President Barack Obama

Dear Barack,

I'm not sure, here in December of 2011, if I should be sending you a Christmas card—or a sympathy card. It's been a tough year to be the man in charge and to live in that bustling-but-lonely white house on Pennsylvania Avenue. The election triumph of 2008 feels like a long time ago, and it's a new and hostile culture now where people don't mind hoisting a mean-spirited sign or telling pollsters just what they think of President Obama's handling of the economy. Americans can say some pretty cruel things in these new "tweets"; it's amazing how much venom can be packed into 140 characters.

So let Me put My main message right up front in the opening paragraphs of this holiday card. You're My child and I love you. And I don't love you just because it's My divine duty, because, you know, "God loves everybody." I don't have to force love; I really do love you, and your beautiful, poised First Lady, Michelle, and your daughters, Malia and Sasha. I'm your heavenly Father, and I go through all the emotions an earthly dad does—pride, supportiveness, sympathetic frustration when you have failures, endless forgiveness, eagerness to share in your life, and a steadfast belief in you and your potential. I know your heart like no commentator or protester ever could. No one but your own wife and your Father in heaven can know all of the insults you've quietly set to the side, the racial taunts to which you've been exposed. But heaven has a good record of your many soft answers that have turned away wrath.

You found out early on that it's tough to be under scrutiny every single moment of the day and night. Every table ever prepared for you is in the presence of your enemies. Somebody is aiming a cheap cell phone camera at you 24/7, breathlessly hoping for flubs, for dirt, for anything to derail you.

So please keep in mind that I hear every syllable, too, but through the lens of loving you and being your faithful Friend. I honestly think Christians sometimes forget that their Dad in heaven really does know all things. And omnipresence is one of the best things about being God, that way I can be present at more than one maternity ward at a time! Yes, I was there when you were born. And My people, both Republican and Democrat, should remember that when they pass things along that they suspect in their hearts are false.

But what a nice thing it was to watch you grow and slowly mature, to witness the mosaic of people who came along and shaped your life. All of us in heaven knew, of course, that this was America's future forty-fourth president down there on the crowded streets of Indonesia, a skinny mixed-race kid attending school, and later while going through the unwise experimentation with drugs, which you yourself admitted was a great moral failure, then growing and struggling to find yourself at college. And then, one by one, the string of victories that put you in the not very comfortable Oval Office chair you now occupy.

All of this leads to an important thing, Mr. President, about Me and how I relate to presidents, and to kings and prime ministers, and to Middle Eastern dictators who are digging in their heels and setting their security forces against the swelling tide of freedom and change. In just a few weeks, you and the Republicans will be facing the Iowa caucuses and the New Hampshire primary. Are you going to win a second term or get sent packing next November? I already know, and I'm not telling.

There is great danger in the false idea that I'm a part of one political party or the other one. Clearly, that's not true. Both sides mess up, often with disheartening consistency. But when people get it into their minds that A equals B, that being a Christian also means being a member of this or that party, then a kind of bad algebra error can happen in which they decide that B equals A as well. "Hey, since I reliably vote this particular way, I must be in good standing with heaven."

But the plain fact regarding the forty-four presidencies up till now is this: here in heaven, I face the same political reality you do, Barack. I can't make everybody in the world do certain things. That's just not My way. It never has been; it never will be. People have free will; and through them, so do many nations. So there's only a certain very limited way in which a United States president is a "leader chosen by God."

What I choose or ordain is the structure and the peace and the quiet orderliness that a nation experiences by having a government. Government is a godly principle. It allows men and women the liberty to *be,* to thrive, to develop initiative and character, to work and play and worship—or decide that they really don't want to worship. (I love that First Amendment.) Government enables a people to protect themselves; it gives them a hopefully efficient and sensitive mechanism for providing temporary assistance to those among them who are struggling after a hurricane or are without jobs.

So the idea of a president of the United States is godly

and it's biblical and it's supported by the plain words of Scripture. Romans 13 says, Pay your taxes. Obey elected officials. Honor and respect those who have been placed over you by the ballots of your peers. When a president of the United States puts his or her hand on the Bible to take the oath of office, he or she is My chosen leader in the sense that I choose that there should *be* leaders. Because I want all My children, religious and otherwise, to have a good framework of a government led by wise and noble people.

But did I get out a ballot of My own in 2008 and say to all the angels, "I pick Obama over McCain"? And two years later, undo all that by picking Tea Party candidates over all their opponents? In 1968, did I pull cosmic levers and put Nixon in ahead of Humphrey and subject America to the long scourge of Watergate? Going back quite a few years, was I, God, a card-carrying member of the Whig Party? Did I pour myself into the 1840 presidential campaign, helping William Henry Harrison get the best of Van Buren, only for Harrison to give such a long inaugural speech in the cold of D.C. that he died of pneumonia thirty-two days later, sparking a constitutional crisis? Am I that inept a Deity?

The point is this, and I say it to you, Mr. President, and to the people who will follow you into the highest office of the land. Be careful, candidates, about saying that you're My choice. My will is already made plain in Scripture: stable governments, freedom from oppression, care for the widows, security, and prosperity. But when people tell CNN, "Now listen, God especially chose me to run this race," and then they lose by twenty points, genuine people of God lose some of their credibility.

Let Me share a word of exhortation to you and also to the Romneys and Perrys and Bachmanns and Boehners of the world. This is for you, Barack, and also for your detractors. Many good people can see things differently and still love their country—and still unite with an eye toward the bigger goals of your nation. There's party, and then there's country. Which is more important? There's winning, and then there's blessing the people with the four years of building and opportunity that winning is supposed to give you.

Not too long ago, you invested a few hours in a quick plane trip overseas, hoping you could bring the 2016 Olympic Games to the United States. Well, it didn't happen. The Summer Games can't be in Rio de Janeiro and Chicago at the same time. Only one national leader can fly home with the trophy. It turned out not to be you. But there were those in the United States who, while loving their country and being the types who would have rooted robustly for American athletes, were openly celebrating your failure. Why? Because they got things a bit upside down. At least momentarily, their dislike of you outweighed their love for America. And I think your side, Barack, is capable of the same.

When I sent My own Son down to earth two thousand years ago—you know, the Christ child in the manger—He was invited to simply win cheap. His opponent across the aisle said, "Worship me for five seconds. You don't even have to mean it. And I'll give You what you want." But Jesus came to your world with a larger purpose. In the Garden of Gethsemane, He didn't want to go to the cross. One disciple betrayed Him; one denied Him; the other ten all took off. The entire nation turned against Him. The streets were lined with people shouting out, "Crucify Him!" Talk about a shellacking at the polls. But He knew what He and I both wanted—a lasting government that would stand and protect and serve and comfort for all time. So He made cosmic decisions instead of just easy ones.

Barack, since some folks from both parties are taking a break from their Christmas rush to listen in, let Me say a word to them too. Folks, you're to love this man. You don't have to vote for him. You don't have to agree with him. You can go all out to give money to the other side and, next November, walk to a precinct and volunteer at a phone bank in order to beat him and replace him with someone you prefer. But if you claim to be a servant of My Son, then you're expected to pray for the president and to love him. Democrats, you were supposed to love and pray for George W. Bush—did you remember to do that?

One of My treasured friends and devoted servants is a pastor named Ed Dobson. He used to be a high-ranking and bossy lieutenant in the Moral Majority, until he came under the conviction that there's a more grace-oriented and loving way to transform a hurting world. He wrote a book entitled *Blinded by Might,* leaving behind the politics of hate and division and coded rhetoric. And he began to suggest that the mandate for the Christian was to love and pray for elected officials, even when they disappoint. He borrowed a line from Paul Ramsey: " 'Call no man vile for whom Christ died.' "

A certain president from Arkansas ended up with some very public sin issues. The Christian world was in great distress, and some of the Christians paraded around with placards that didn't reflect the values of heaven. But the Sunday after this tragic, ugly story broke, Pastor Dobson, the former activist for the religious right, climbed into his pulpit and prayed for President Clinton. He prayed to thank Me for America's freedoms—for the right to worship. He prayed for an extra measure of courage and understanding for his congregation. And then he asked Me to encourage Hillary and Chelsea. He asked Me to wrap My arms of love and grace around that bruised and beaten-down family. He put in his prayer a biblical line from John 8 about who should cast stones first.

Well, friend of Mine, I have other letters to get in the mail. This is My busy time, as you know. But here in this Christmas season, Barack, I want you to take heart. Polls are not the big thing; serving others is the big thing. And you do that rather well. Every day, get up and do good for the people. Love them and lead them. They often pray for you, and I do hear them. And I also hear and respond when you pray for them.

Merry Christmas.

Love,
God

God's *Christmas* CARD TO
Jaycee Dugard

Dear Jaycee,

This is God. You remember, " 'I see the moon and the moon sees me, God bless the moon, and God bless me.' " During the 6,646 days when you were in captivity, you so often looked out of that tent and saw the moon. The moon was your connection to your mother. You hoped she was looking up through her tears and seeing the same moon you did. But from the moment you were dragged into that car and covered up with a blanket until you gained your freedom eighteen terrible years later, the moon always saw you and I always saw you too. I never once left; I never once stepped away. I know it's hard to understand how a God who "loves little children" could just watch and do nothing. The answer isn't easy or simple, but it's true and real. Just like My love.

Jaycee, you have every right to ask Me some very hard questions. But first I want to say something to you. I love you so much. I loved you on the day you were born. I was there and loved you when you lost your first tooth. I was there and loved you when your little sister Shayna joined the family. And yes, I was right there with you as you walked up the road on the way to school on June 10, 1991.

In your book, *A Stolen Life,* you say, "I don't believe in hate." You say that you've forgiven the craven, evil man who stole you. But at the same time, I can certainly understand if you were to respond to My "I love yous" with a flood of cynical tears. Because what did God's love ever do for you? During those years, when you were chained to this monster's bed, you once made a list of the ten things you cared most about. And the highest on your list was this: "Knowing someone loves me." You also wrote that all good fathers have "genuine love for their children." Well, Jaycee, I do love you with all of My heart, and I want to offer you all of the joy and peace and love your heart can hold. I want to offer you such happiness that the pain of what happened to you will fade away like mist.

It's a terrible, painful thing, Jaycee, to be present at the scene of a crime, and not reach out and prevent it. I have stood to the side time after time after time as people have been raped and tortured and killed. I could have stricken your kidnappers with a flat tire. I could have reached out My hand and taken away his stun gun. I could have made him choke on a pretzel in prison during his earlier sentence as a sex offender. I could have simply touched him with My finger and made him disappear forever; knowing the evil in his heart, few in the universe would have objected. But I didn't. I didn't do any of those things. And maybe, now that you've been rescued and are a beautiful, articulate young adult, you can begin to understand why.

At the close of time, the Bible talks about a thousand-year period called the millennium. What happens then? "Books are opened," it says in Revelation (see Revelation 20:12). The judgment is going to take place. And I will probably stand trial more than any of My subjects. What do I have to say for Myself? I might have to spend the entire one thousand years simply addressing the whole universe, all of assembled humanity, regarding the case of Jaycee Lee Dugard and the cases of so many others who suffered. And I'll take all those years, as long as it requires, to painfully explain why the terrible story of sin had to unfold this way, to reveal the entire panorama of evil and rebellion and the detour away from Eden—and why it was that you and all humans were caught in such a terrible trap.

You see, before I even stepped out into deep space and said, "Let there be light," I already planned that you would be here (Genesis 1:3). I knew your name the same day I knew Adam's and Eve's names. Centuries beforehand, I thought you were a great kid and I smiled every time I thought about it.

And, of course, My plan was perfect. In My plan, you'd grow up. You'd be happy. You'd love your animals and your sister and your family. You'd love the winter sports in Tahoe and the summers playing under the trees. And one wonderful day you'd meet a handsome man and marry him. Together you'd make babies and love them until your heart almost burst with joy.

That was My plan. I had a plan like that for Adam and Eve too. If they just kept on loving Me and believing Me and enjoying our weekly visits in the Garden, it would have unfolded that way, right down to the end of time.

But then I could see a fairly small, almost imperceptible crime about to take place. Lucifer was speaking with Eve, and she listened to him. I didn't want her to, but she did. The inescapable truth is that even I, God, don't get to have everything in the universe My way. She disobeyed the most elementary rule of heaven, and turned away from this wonderful, cosmic blueprint that would have been endlessly perfect.

And I had a choice. I could reach out with My own stun gun and zap that serpent in the tree. I could put a burning bush in the path, and frighten Eve back to her senses. I could actually reach out and hold her tightly by the wrist. In other words, I could have—in a way—made Eve a prisoner. I could have put her and her children in handcuffs and built a tall fence that kept them on the safe side of the river of life forever. But when you don't allow people the freedom to do what they choose to do, something happens to the entire galactic plan. I certainly have the power to make everyone good. And someday soon everyone *will* be good; but not because I forced them to be.

Life on earth began to twist and churn. When Adam and Eve had children, I had to stand back and allow the first child born on the soil of earth to kill the second one. The high cost of free will was beginning to be seen. It wasn't what I wanted, but the rebellion—the choice to follow Satan and selfishness—had to run its entire course. I stayed on the sidelines and witnessed an almost unfathomable amount of pain and loss every year, all the way down to 1991, when your life took such a tragic turn.

I would have done anything to save you from that pain, Jaycee—anything—except turn all humans into robotic prisoners of My will, anything, except condemn the whole universe to never-ending pain and death. What I did do was send My own Son to pay the price for sin on the cross, so that you and all who choose unselfishness and love can have never-ending lives of joy. Nothing on earth can make up for what was done to you—no amount of money will make it right. But I believe in freedom—and I'm going to bear the full cost of making it permanent, beginning with the cross on Calvary.

Jaycee, the title of your book is so true: *A Stolen Life.* This man and his wife stole your life. They stole you from your mother. They stole your eighth-grade graduation. They stole your high school years. You write how they stole your first crush, your first date, the thrill of going down to the DMV and getting your first driver's license. It was sweet to read how, finally, when you got out, your baby sister, who was only one and a half when you were taken away, *she* taught you how to drive and celebrated with you when you put that laminated card in your purse for the first time. But these people stole your life.

And when the curtain comes down on this terrible but necessary drama, Jaycee, here's what I promise to do. I want to do it, and I *will* do it: I am going to give you back everything that was taken. I will restore what your enemy took away. I will restore what has been stolen from all humans.

This criminal being took away your childhood, those eighteen precious, irreplaceable, vulnerable years. But I will give them back *in full;* I will provide for you a paradise that has no end, where the birthdays just keep on coming. That's not metaphor and that's not a poem or a memory verse; that is the pure, hard, rock-solid truth. In My kingdom, My children live forever. Life without end.

This man and his partner in crime stole your name. For eighteen years, you could never write or speak the name *Jaycee.* They forced you to call yourself Allissa. Over and over, you had to lie to people about your name and your identity and who you were. But I always knew your name and whispered it to Myself as I saw you surviving there in the shadows of that hard, lonely life. Your name is already engraved on a mansion here in heaven. If you wish, you can write it again on every wall.

This criminal, unbalanced and evil as he was, spouted endless wearying bits of garbage about "angels." He was always hearing voices urging sinister plots. God was making him do this or that. His angels were craven, diabolical enemies, his partners in these crimes.

But when you get here, Jaycee, you're going to meet the

wonderful legions of friendly, caring angels, all created by Me, and all ready to surround your life with warm and healing perfection. These wonderful, winged friends delight to do as I ask, and all I ask is that they bring hope and happiness everywhere they go. You'll love them, and they already love you.

Jaycee, you suffered the worst sort of abuse in your captivity. I promise that heaven will be filled with loving relationships. You will love and be loved. I will see to it. No one will ever take your two wonderful daughters away from you. What was taken away will be given back; I, God, make you that promise. I will turn darkness into light. Already now, you see that your own two girls, born in the midst of tragedy, are bright, amazing children, worthy of a mother's love and a heavenly Father's pride. One more thing: even as God, I'm thankful that heaven is forever, ten thousand years and far, far beyond, because I feel like My own kingdom owes you so much. You deserve the infinity that is waiting here for you.

For 6,646 days, you lost your freedom. That man kept you in handcuffs. Then he forced you into a tiny shed where there was a lock on the door. He threatened you by saying there were fierce dogs in the yard: "Don't even think of stepping outside." Even when you had the chance to surf the Internet, he drilled it into your mind: "I'm watching everything you do." You couldn't try to track down your mother because you were convinced he was spying on every keystroke. I think about that line in your book: "I still could not crash through the wall that he built *inside of me.*"

As the years passed, he used his twisted mind games to exert total control. After a while, even without handcuffs, you were still a prisoner. You wouldn't have known how to escape even if the opportunity had presented itself.

So My gift to you, Jaycee, includes this: absolute, wonderful, unfettered freedom. For a million years and forever, you can live in a kingdom with no walls. No fences. No locks. You and your daughters and friends can travel to distant galaxies. No one will ask you to check in; there won't be curfews. When you gained your freedom, you wrote, you were even afraid to go and buy gas at first. None of that here! Come and go; stay out late; sleep in. Bask in the pure, untainted liberty that is going to always be the hallmark of the restored universe once Satan is forever gone.

It's only right that you should wonder about what will happen to your kidnapper. The state of California decided to punish him with 431 years in prison. So there he is, locked away behind bars where he belongs. Is that enough?

My own Son, Jesus, once considered a nice girl, perhaps about your age, and then said to those around Him, "If you mess with an innocent child like this one, do yourself and us a favor. Get a millstone, hang it around your own neck, and then drown yourself. Because that will be easier than what is going to come your way when I return to planet Earth to give out rewards and punishments" (see Matthew 18:6).

It is a demonstration of your great heart, Jaycee, that even without My knowledge of how he became the twisted animal he is, you have forgiven your kidnapper. My heart also breaks for who he could have been. His eternal destiny is not the subject of this card. But know that justice and fairness are as important to Me as free will.

I make you this promise, Jaycee: in My eternity, those who hurt the innocent will be *gone*. They will not be here any longer. You will be able to take your children by the hand and fly through the stars, a trillion miles in any direction, and never see a trace of hatred or meanness or suffering ever again. They will be completely gone forever.

"Behold, I make all things new" (Revelation 21:5; emphasis added). Especially for you. Merry Christmas, My dear child, Jaycee.

Love forever,
God

God's *Christmas* CARD TO
John Edwards

Dear John,

Well, like it says in My book, 2 Samuel 1:25, *"How the mighty have fallen"* (NIV; emphasis added). And those five words pretty much sum up your career and your entire life: millionaire trial lawyer, then senator, then vice presidential candidate, then presidential candidate—and then the scandalous headlines. As I get ready to take this card over to the post office, there's actually a chance that you could get handcuffed, be forced to put on an orange jumpsuit, and serve prison time on six federal counts of conspiracy, taking illegal contributions, and perjuring yourself. How can a man with everything going for him think it would be all right to have an affair while his own wife is dying of cancer?

Nothing is harder for Me than when one of My children, one of My beloved, has a spectacular fall. A crash. I've been through it before, I'll go through it again, and when December comes, I still send a Christmas card out to a man who remains in My heart and My future plans. So Merry Christmas to you, My child and My friend, John Edwards.

I just sent a card to President Obama. He's the man who got all of the things you wanted. Today, he's living in the White House you wanted to inherit. You wanted so badly to get the keys to Air Force One and to have Secret Service details around you 24/7. Somewhere along the road, the down-to-earth guy, the aw-shucks son of a textile mill worker, the blue-collar hero, who wanted to make antipoverty his overriding campaign theme, lost his way. The trappings of power and the perks of fame became a fast-growing cancer and they destroyed you.

I have some redemptive, good news for you, John. A wise statesman, like any thoughtful Christian, can examine his own life story and find comfort and healing in how I've dealt with others in similar circumstances. The stories in the Bible—the good, the bad, and the ugly, the uplifting and the scandal ridden—are all recorded and shared for the saving of My people. First Corinthians 10:6 makes it clear: *These are all warning markers*—danger!—*in our history books, written down so that we don't repeat their mistakes.* I've sent this message to others in the form of a Christmas card, so I can say that there is hope and a future still for you.

Really, we've all heard your story before. A powerful leader becomes infatuated by a beautiful woman. He falls into a liaison. The woman gets pregnant. The powerful man tries to pull strings to cover it all up. When that doesn't work, he attempts a bit of misdirection, makes a clumsy attempt to establish someone else as the baby's father. Inevitably, some within the inner circle uncover the mess, and one of them has to confront the powerful man. That doesn't go well at all, and the big shot's initial reaction is bluster and denial and outright lies.

So, does any of this sound familiar, John? Of course, I'm talking about My fallen and restored chosen monarch, King David. The woman's name is Bathsheba. The fall guy is her own husband, Uriah. The intervention leader is the prophet Nathan.

And here, three thousand years later, is what can basically be described as a Hollywood remake. You knew this

Bible story from Sunday School, and man, you went out and did the exact same thing. Practically nothing has changed except that it's airplanes instead of chariots. Otherwise, the story is distressingly, almost eerily similar.

You begin as a good senator, a public servant who really does seem to care about those who are down-and-out. Even though you personally are a multimillionaire, you tell campaign aides that poverty is your top issue, and you actually mean it. Someone asks, "What's the one best word to describe John Edwards?" and the reply is, "Nice." And it's true! You care about others. When your own boy, Wade, is killed in a car crash (I wept with you that day), friends see the anguish, the vulnerable humanity that you and Elizabeth exhibit. It's enough to almost get Al Gore to pick you for vice president in 2000 and, four years later, John Kerry *does* ask you to be his running mate.

And then something happens inside of you. There are people who can hold power and use it to help others while staying humble themselves. They never forget that kingdoms exist for the people, not the kings, that the concept of government is biblical *and* should be focused always on service and self-sacrifice and doing for others. The White House is supposed to be the place where needs find solutions and where the hurts of society are addressed and solved.

But all at once, you begin to really enjoy riding on that campaign plane and having gofers all around who jump when you snap your fingers. You go from saying with surprised and humble pleasure, "They love me," to saying with a cynical smirk, "They *looooove* me!" You quickly grow disdainful of the more humble, day-to-day events where it's just you and fifteen country bumpkin diners in a coffee shop. If each event isn't in a jam-packed stadium or a ritzy ballroom, well, you aren't interested. You have a lot of staffers available to do your dirty work, and you become a bit disdainful, bossing them here and there. On the rare occasions where you have to fly commercial—and by now it has to be first class or forget it—you order some flunky to find out which movies are being shown on the plane and to change schedules if you've already seen them. Little things like that, which really began to add up.

The very day you and Kerry lose that presidential race, two things happen. You and Elizabeth find out she has cancer. And you decide that you're running for president again. You and your friends begin gaming out the next four years and the 2008 race. You'll have to run to the left of Hillary Clinton, you realize. You'll have to be the common man, the Main Street guy, the "nice" candidate who cares about those who have been left behind. But by now you do like those big, comfortable seats on the private jets your corporate friends loan to you. You begin construction on a twenty-eight-thousand-square-foot house "for Elizabeth," you tell everybody. "She's not well; she deserves it." But the fact is that you've begun to fall seriously in love with yourself—*narcissism* is what the psychological therapists call it—and you want and are sure you deserve all of these things. Especially that very comfortable and powerful chair in an oval-shaped office back east.

And then comes your own Bathsheba temptress. Truth be told, Bathsheba was just taking a bath on a nearby rooftop, minding her own business. But this dangerous-looking woman picks you out and stalks you for her own purposes. There, in an exclusive bar of the Regency Hotel, she hits on you. " 'My friends insist you're John Edwards,' sa Hunter. 'I tell them no way—you're way too han And John, as cheesy and sophomoric and self-e that line is, you fall for it. Your aide, Josh Brumberger, tries to shield you, to fend her off for your sake and for the sake of the cause, the campaign.

But she talks her way onto the campaign as a video producer. She'll capture the real John Edwards, she promises you. Day after exciting day, she'll post disarming, winsome videos on the Web, attracting huge crowds of supporters. She can put you in the White House; she's sure of it. And the flattery, aided by her perfume and seductive lashes, is just too much for you. "You're so real. You're another Martin Luther King Junior, another Gandhi." No wonder King David's own son, Solomon, once lamented, "A flattering mouth works ruin" (Proverbs 26:28, NIV). Before long, she's a fixture on the road with you, sharing plane rides, limos, and yes, hotel suites.

Campaign staffers see the video pieces and are appalled at the flirtatious tone, the wanton air of risqué closeness. Very quickly, key aides assume the worst and know that someone has to come to you. That same young man, Josh, knocks on your hotel door during a stop in Ohio. "Senator, it doesn't look good. People are making all sorts of assumptions. We're in the perception game, and perception becomes reality in this business." You act surprised, profess total innocence, but tell him you'll take care of it.

But in truth, you're unrepentant; the saga continues. Another aide comes to you and basically says, "Thou art the man!" You blow him off as well. And one day, you call Josh over once again and chew him out from South Carolina to Maine and back. "This is all your fault," you shout at him. "All these stories going around. You're off the team; you're fired."

So this young man, white-faced with agonized distress, manages to say, "I'm sorry you feel this way. I honestly just wanted to help make you the next president of the United States."

And this is the line, John, that hurts the most. You say to this young man, "Why didn't you stop me? Why didn't you come to me?"

"I did talk to you," he blurts out. "Right after Labor Day. In Ohio."

And in crude language not fit for God's people to bear, John, you say to him, "No, you should have come to me *stronger*—and somehow kept me from doing what I was doing." You, John Edwards, a man who wanted to be leader of the free world, a man who would put his hand on the Bible and then take responsibility for the lives of 310 million others—you wanted this young political aide to be a moral policeman, to tie your own hands behind you and make you behave yourself.

Well, the woman gets pregnant. You and Elizabeth scheme to have a friend, Andrew Young, take the fall and say the baby is his. Fortunately, you lose in Iowa. Meanwhile, your own campaign team has agonized for months. Do they have a responsibility to turn you in, to report what they know? What if they keep quiet, and somehow you win those caucuses and vault your way to the Democratic nomination? What if you get clear to Washington, and then have a scarlet mess like this explode?

So now it's Christmas. Elizabeth succumbed to her disease. You're alone with your haunted memories, with your own personal demons. I know that your marriage was a rocky, often wrenching saga all its own. She bore things; you bore things. It was harder for you than people realize. And here you are on the jagged rocks, still with three children, and with government men holding indictments parked on your doorstep.

So what can I say to you, John Edwards, My friend who will never enjoy the heady title of Mr. President? What is God's Christmas card to you here in 2011?

First, I love you. I love you so much, John. This was agony for Me to experience. Your dreams were shattering, and your own foolhardiness was causing you and others such pain. When your friends wept, I wept too. It was a tragedy on all counts, and I was sorry for what sin was doing to the Edwards family.

But even here in hindsight, as you look back and shake your own head in disbelief, I can tell you this, John: forgiveness is yours. For all that you did, if you wish it, I forgive you. I can wipe it clean. I can pardon your affair and your lies and your treachery. I can give you a new start and the guarantee of a heavenly mansion better than the nice house located at 1600 Pennsylvania Avenue.

Some people are aghast even to this day that I forgave King David. I mean, he went further than you did; he conspired to have someone killed in battle just to cover his tracks and throw MSNBC off the trail. But I forgave him. He pled with Me in Psalm 51 and there was anguish in every word: *"Have mercy on me. Blot it out. Wash it away. Cleanse me with hyssop. Make me whiter than snow. Create in me a new heart. Renew a right spirit within me."* That man was in agony; but when he came to Me, he found that it was enough. Even the faintest promise of a future Calvary was enough.

Now there was still a price to be paid for such blatant folly. David was a weakened king thereafter, a man with compromised influence. It was a devastating moment for Me, but John, I allowed the infant son born of that liaison to perish. That sounds cruel and vindictive on My part, but the stark, awful truth is that when powerful men lie and murder and deceive, many, many innocent people in their wake take the knife in the heart. And this one time, I wanted for all My people to mark that bloody lesson and never forget it.

You could have been a great president, John Edwards. You could have attacked poverty at its roots. You could have fought for justice and for jobs and for dignified lives for the poor and broken. That didn't happen because of your selfish choices, and the Wall Street numbers bear out what I'm saying. Forgiveness is free, but our mistakes can be oh, so expensive.

One last point, John. My beloved, fragile, well-meaning but impetuous friend David found healing and restoration because he sought it with every bit of his breaking heart. There was a moment when he blustered. He tried to stonewall his cabinet, and then he tried to dodge the pointed finger of the prophet Nathan. But at last, in 2 Samuel 12:13, he uttered those six devastating but necessary words: "I have sinned against the LORD" (NIV).

There could still be a future for you, John. You could still do good. You could rise again and redeem the promises you made to your legions of hopeful fans and supporters. But first comes the moment of confession and contrition. No lawyer tricks. No change of venue. No evading justice on technicalities. No taking the Fifth. Instead, "I have sinned. I want to be cleansed. I want to sacrifice my ego, my messianic ambitions, my thirst for pleasure and power. Father God, I want nothing anymore but to be Your child and Your humble servant again."

I still remember so acutely when King David was broken—and then made well. Paul also, laid in the dust outside Damascus, blind and shattered. He rose up to become My finest apostle. Peter was a demolished man after Gethsemane;

his heartbreak when he denied Jesus three times is grief you can't even fathom. My Son and I forgave him and he accomplished herculean things for Heaven. In My eternal providence, Christmas Day is followed by a new year, and, once again, I hope, a new man.

Merry Christmas, John.

Love,
God

God's *Christmas* CARD TO
Bernie Madoff

Dear Bernie,

I actually have to address this Christmas card to Inmate 61727-054; otherwise, the postal service will never get it to you. Because, after many years of living high on other people's money—houses in Manhattan, a chalet in France, a mansion in Palm Beach, a fifty-five-foot yacht—and wearing expensive designer suits, you're now clad in the prison garb of a federal correctional institution. And what's a nice guy like you doing in prison? Over the span of twenty years, you methodically and deviously stole somewhere in the neighborhood of sixty-five billion dollars.

"This is off the charts," the judge said at the end of the trial. He sidestepped the fact that you were already seventy-one years old and sentenced you to the maximum of 150 years behind bars. People who have a sense of humor—and that would have to be folks who weren't personally ripped off by you and your family—smiled when they figured that even with good behavior, you won't be out riding on your yacht again until somewhere 2159, when you would be 211 years old.

I never send a rebuke, Bernie, without also offering redemption, and My heart yearns to give you healing today. But first I have to sit across from you with that thick plexiglass separating us, and simply shake My head in grief. To walk, eyes wide open, into a life of white-collar crime, stealing from trusting people, taking their money and using it to fool other people into investing—you became a destroyer of lives.

It's ironic that in your first job, you were a lifeguard. You looked out for people in trouble and you saved them. You rescued people who needed help. But you took the five thousand dollars you made at the beach, learned how to buy penny stocks, and it didn't take long before you were the head of Bernard L. Madoff Investment Securities, LLC. Even back in the sixties, you were bright enough to use computers to help you get ahead of your competition; some credit you with being one of the founders of the entire NASDAQ exchange system.

Even from your beginning forays into the vast casino of the stock market, you played on the edges of honesty. You set up a system that basically bribed brokers to send inexperienced stock players your way. You took advantage of them to the full extent of the law—and then crossed over into the criminal.

There's a Bible parable My Son liked to tell, and Matthew finally wrote it down in chapter 18 of his book. A man ran up a massive debt: ten thousand talents. In those days, it was a vast, enormous debt, like the amount of money you eventually took from people. And the good news of that parable is that the man was forgiven—just as you can be forgiven, Bernie. Grace is a ceaseless river that flows from Calvary, and it's sufficient for this loss. What Jesus did for the human race at Calvary is an ample account to make up for your theft. "Behold! The Lamb of God," His cousin John once said, "who takes away the sin of the world" (John 1:29, NKJV).

One aspect of My Son's story is that this man who owed billions of dollars simply wasn't able to pay it back. This is certainly true of you, Bernie. Beginning around 1990, you began taking money from people, from corporations, from charitable foundations, and you promised to invest it wisely.

God's Christmas Card to Bernie Madoff

You could guarantee them spectacular returns because you were Bernie Madoff; you were the wizard with the Midas touch. But the plain fact was that you simply took those swimming pools full of hundred-dollar bills and shoved them into a bank account. You didn't invest them; you never intended to invest them. You simply pretended to invest them. Every now and then, you would take new money out and pay some of the earlier investors. You gave a whole new meaning to the phrase "rob Peter to pay Paul."

The actual reality is that about thirty-six billion dollars got poured into the scam, and sixty-five billion dollars were lost based on what you promised investors would make. Approximately half of those dollars got paid back to a lucky few people, the other eighteen billion dollars simply melted away into Madoffville and the Madoff lifestyle. Between you and your family, the money was gone. And how can you pay it back when you're in jail? Your life now illustrates the tragic reality of how powerless a sinner is to make good on his failures.

Yes, some people had been suspicious of you. Many more should have been. Which is something I need to say to the rest of my children: folks, if something seems too good to be true, it generally is. There aren't any widows in Nigeria who need your help in getting their fifteen million dollars out of the country; there just aren't. Please, be as harmless as doves, but also as wise as serpents (Matthew 10:16). As C. S. Lewis once put it, God "wants a child's heart, but a grown-up's head. He wants us to be simple, single-minded, affectionate, and teachable, as good children are; but He also wants every bit of intelligence we have to be alert at its job, and in first class fighting trim."

Finally, the day came when you confessed to your family that not only was there not enough money to pay off investors—the whole thing had been a massive lie from the beginning. Your own sons reported you to the federal authorities.

And here's the point that goes back to that Bible parable. You couldn't scrape and earn back that eighteen billion dollars even if you were free and working hard back on Wall Street. You certainly can't make good when you're incarcerated and making nine cents an hour in the prison laundry. Most of the money is simply—gone. When you were sentenced, you said to your victims, "I'll live with this the rest of my life. I'm sorry." Then, realizing that talk is cheap, you added, "I know that doesn't help you." It broke My heart to see the pain that you had caused. Finally, I think, it broke yours too.

This brings us to the stark reality of the Christmas message and the gospel. You're in a hopeless situation, My friend. You owe this massive debt and you're never going to be able to pay it back. And yet, because of the Christ child, because of what My Son, Jesus, did on the cross, you can be offered forgiveness—full and free—a complete canceling of the debt, an erasing of the entire sad saga. Gone. Forgiven. Pardoned. Set free. A new beginning. This is the message of Christmas.

A great debate goes on in theological circles about the morality of a heavenly Father forgiving His broken and rebellious children: people like you, Bernie. Is it righteous for God to forgive cold, calculating sins? Monumental crimes against humanity? In the book *The Sunflower,* Simon Wiesenthal wrestles with the dilemma of the Nazi guard who had committed atrocities during World War II. He had helped to torture and burn alive more than a hundred Jews. Now, on his deathbed, he wanted a Jew, any Jew, to say, "I forgive you." Could Simon be that man?

Could he say the words that would let this tormented German guard find some emotional relief? Simon looked at him, his own heart aching with anger, and finally walked out of the room without a word. Cynthia Ozick, later hearing the story, remarked, "Let the SS man die unshriven. Let him go to hell."

But you see, the miracle of Calvary is that Jesus offered up the ultimate Sacrifice, the investment, so to speak, that is sufficient to stand for all of the sins of the world. Heaven doesn't ignore sins; it doesn't sweep them aside; it doesn't pretend the wrenching losses didn't pile up; it doesn't dispute an estimated loss of sixty-five billion dollars. But I can tell you that the agony My Son and I endured when He went up on that cross, and the blood He shed up there, was sufficient to offer forgiveness for any sin, payment for any debt.

Mark 2 tells about a day when Jesus was telling gospel stories in someone's house. A big crowd had gathered around the house to listen—so many people that four friends carrying a paralyzed man couldn't even get close to Jesus. So they carried him up to the roof, cut a hole, and let him right down into the middle of the prayer meeting. When Jesus saw him, He knew that the man's broken body wasn't the main reason he had dropped in. The man was really sick with guilt about things he had done wrong. Jesus quietly said to him, "Son, your sins are forgiven you" (verse 5, NKJV).

Immediately, the lawyers and religious leaders in the room began to mutter, "What's all this? 'I forgive you'? On what basis? Who gives You the right? This man didn't sin against *You*, Jesus. You have no moral standing to forgive." But the fact was that Jesus, My Son, was fully God. He had the right to forgive any sins He wanted to—especially with the cosmic reality that Calvary, a still future but planned, premeditated, calculated paying of this planet's price tag of sin, was just about to happen.

In this particular story, you stole other people's money. It's gone. Is it moral for Jesus to step forward and say to you, "Forgiveness is yours"? Is that right? Does Calvary have an insensitivity to the debt you owe other people? No, because Jesus offers healing and restoration to them as well. Because of you, people lost their fortunes and they suffered from the loss. But the Christ child is equally My gift to them too. Their losses and hurts and resentments can be fully made up with a heavenly mansion and an eternity in a heavenly place where these injustices will be a gently fading memory.

So this is where you are, Inmate 61727-054. You're not just a number to Me, though, Bernie; you're My friend and you're My child and I love you. I'm with you there in jail on this cold December day. But here at Christmas, your only hope is Me. There's nothing else and no one else. I want to be your Father and your Friend; I want for My Son to be your Redeemer and your Savior.

My beloved friend, Tony Evans, once imagined coming to Judgment Day, just as you had to when you faced a judge. And Tony tried to imagine what he might be able to say in order to get his accounts square, to get right with Me. Frankly, he hadn't lived nearly so desperate a life as you have. He was just a nickel-and-dime sinner—not one of the sixty-five-billion-dollar variety. But his classic line is this: "I'd say, 'Jesus, there's a list of sins in that book right there. And I'm guilty on every count. But when I was eleven years old, I got down on my knees and told You that I was a sinner. I told You I believe that when You died on that cross, You died for me. I believe that You have already paid my penalty. And Jesus, *You are all I have*!'"

God's Christmas Card to Bernie Madoff

Bernie, I'm all you have—Me and My Son, the Babe in the manger and the Lamb slain for your sins. He's back with Me now, though, and if you say Yes, We're ready to be your Legal Team. And what We've got for you is more than enough.

Merry Christmas, My friend.

Love,
God

God's *Christmas* CARD TO
You

Dear You,

I know how often you get mail, even Christmas cards, addressed just to "Occupant." Or a piece of junk mail where a politician's computer pretends that it knows you. They digitally sprinkle your first name here and there in the copy, and sometimes even use an artificial signature machine. And, of course, with Pastor Dan sitting in this chair imagining on My behalf, he *has* to say, "Dear So-and-So." But try to quietly pause here at Christmastime in order to understand this one unshakable truth: *This is not a form letter!* I—God—know you. I'm aware of you. I care about you. And I love you.

That's hard to convey because the Bible is My Word sent to 6.9 billion people. So it seems distant and impersonal. The book of nature is a mass mailing, a group e-mail visible to one and all. I sent Jesus to save the entire world, and that was some two thousand Decembers ago too. The preacher delivers his Christmas homily and says, "God loves you." That sounds generic. John 3:16, *"God so loved the world"* (emphasis added). Generic. *For unto* us *a Child is born.* Generic. Collective. Impersonal.

But gifts really count the best when they come with just one chosen name on the tag. And the everlasting reality is that Jesus and I sat down and We made a plan just for you—a plan to rescue and redeem you, because We cared so very much just about you.

I've been licking stamps, so to speak, for some cards to

more famous people. Maybe you read a few of them—and consider it a Christmas blessing right now to *not* be all that famous! God's Christmas card to Casey Anthony, to Tiger Woods, to Bernie Madoff, and to John Edwards. So I shared some good news about forgiveness and about Calvary and about the possibility of a clean slate and starting over. And the same is true for you, you know. Some of your trials this year are just between you and Me—and let's keep it that way—but I'm here to love you despite your flaws, despite this year's bruises and moments of straying off the safe road. My Son, Jesus, is My personal, hand-wrapped, special-delivery Present just for you this December 25. This expensive present called Calvary has a tag right on it: *"With love from Me to you."*

If I weren't using Pastor Dan as a spokesperson—if I really could come right into your home and visit with you today—I'd be able to say, a million times, "Do you remember that camping trip? You got lost in that big clump of trees, and you prayed, and then your daddy came. Yeah, I was there." "Do you remember when your grandmother was so sick and you and your family were in the hospital for the final vigil? I was there too. You sort of felt My presence, and even though your grandma went to sleep in My arms, I spent those final, precious moments right there with you and your family." "Do you remember that vacation that was so much fun, so perfect, the best one ever? You and your husband traveled to Lake Louise in Alberta, and the high trees and that pristine green water made you think about heaven. I was right there, filling your heart with the wonder of our universe, creating that snowy bit of alpine magic outside your hotel room, just for him and you."

I have so many memories, so many fine moments that were just Me and you. Every Christmas, from the first one you spent on this planet, until this one right now, I've made it a point to savor some holiday time just in your presence—just the two of us.

Now, some people say, "Come on. How's that possible? That's akin to a bit of Santa Claus folklore, in which a man in a big red suit miraculously goes down two billion chimneys in just one night, and presents for all good boys and girls fit into one big bag." Well, I'm not Santa, but there's something wonderful about being God, especially in December. I'm able to be, really *be,* one on one just with you, and that doesn't conflict with My equally close and intimate relationship with your child living in Akron—or an orphan in Chiang Mai, Thailand, or a widow on her deathbed in Peru.

I always thought that my friend C. S. Lewis described My celestial viewpoint pretty well. Being God, he said, is a bit like being an author, and, of course, he would know about that. The writer sits at his desk and types out something such as, "Mary laid down her work; next moment came a knock at the door!"

Now, the writer is putting those words on the paper. Between Mary's setting down of her knitting and going over to turn the knob and saying, "Come on in," he, the author, might stop for several hours and have a sandwich. He might take a whole week off and go on a fishing trip. He might simply sit in that chair and think about "Mary," musing on her character and her personality and her backstory for that whole week. Because for the writer, time simply isn't a problem. He's above the time in the story. He's the master of time. He might be writing three books at the same time, and can give wonderful, personal, intimate, detailed attention and care to each of the characters in those stories.

So it's really true that I can care about you, your friend across the street, all of the people in your church, and—well, everybody everywhere, and it's completely intimate and loving and personal and first-name basis with each one of them. Once, a pastor was sitting on a plane about to taxi out, and was startled to sense that I, God, could hear and pay heed to and process millions of simultaneous prayers coming up from all the runways around the world. And I really can! It's amazing and it's wonderful and it's absolutely real.

King David was a man who probably had a hard time keeping track of all of his subjects, not having a personal BlackBerry or an IRS data bank there in Jerusalem. But he did understand this incredible reality of My close connection just with him. *"Lord, You search me and know me,"* he wrote in his 139th psalm. *"You know when I'm sitting down and when I get back up. You know my thoughts. You know what I'm doing day by day. Before a word comes out of my mouth, You already know what I'm going to say."* And I don't suppose it could have been the Christmas season, since David was at least seven hundred years too early for that, but even this powerful monarch admits being humbly grateful to be personally known by his God. *"Such knowledge is too wonderful for me,"* he writes in closing.

I hope you'll carry this personal Christmas card message with you all through the 366 days of the year 2012. I look forward to each of those days with you. When you pray, it's just an amazing gift; I love it. I can't wait for those moments each day. Please, when you lay in bed and whisper a prayer or are around the dinner table, don't forget that I hear the words and appreciate them. Don't ever say phony things or mechanical things or "expected" things when you pray. I already know your thoughts; why cover them up with clichés about food being good to the nourishment of our bodies? Just imagine that I'm right there, three feet away, and then say what you're really thinking. Blurt it right out.

All this next year, I hope you know that I love seeing you in My house. Sure, I'm with you all week long, 24/7, but there's something incredible for Me when you and your friends come to My sanctuary and ponder the joys of living in My heavenly kingdom or when you sing together and pray together and band together to give and to invest in missions. There's not a single generic dime in My budget; I love every gift and every giver. When the choir sings, I hear every individual voice and also can't help but smile ear to ear as the joint harmonies fill up My heart.

I don't spend a lot of time here in heaven reading through the books that get printed by Zondervan and Pacific Press®, because, well, I know what they say before they go to press. But for the sake of what you relate to, I'll just say that I like how Rick Warren describes Me as having a personal, wonderful plan for your life. You were created for My purpose and My pleasure, and My purposes for you are noble and My pleasure in you is overflowing.

I also like how a departed saint named A. W. Tozer once suggested that God is a Friend who can be known. "God is a Person," he writes in a book about actually pursuing Me, "and, as such, can be cultivated as any person can." If right now you only know Me a little bit, well, you can get to know Me more. I'm right here. I have a heart and a personality and a wonderful life, and people have it in their power to get better acquainted with Me. If you got to know Me better in 2012, that would be wonderful, indeed. It would be a fine New Year's resolution.

In fact, let Me say this. Theologians have discussed and

debated and wondered and pontificated for the last two millennia about who is going to be in heaven. Who will get there? Who will make it? Who will God let through the pearly gates? There's much to say on that topic, and I've sent down instructions and scriptural teachings that are helpful. But the bottom line is this: people will be here who want to be here, people who enjoy being My friend, people who appreciate the old rugged cross. Men and women who, with eyes wide open, are such good friends with Jesus that they determine, "You know, an eternity with Christ as the Head of government, the Ruler of all societies, and the King and Lord of my own life, yes, we could go for that."

The fact is that I'm here. In heaven, you'll see a lot of Me. Jesus is here. After He comes to earth to receive our many friends into Paradise, He will forever be on the throne and He will rule in a wonderful way. Anyone who decides they could savor that and thrive under those elegant parameters, they'll be here. People who don't, will have made other plans, and I must say that I am a gentleman God. I honor the personal wishes of people I respect. So the day is soon coming when all who are living, every person who dwells in that remade world called planet Earth will be good friends. They will enjoy My companionship and I will enjoy theirs.

I hope you know how much it means to Me to sense your love. To know you count it as good news that all of My people are one Christmas closer to heaven. And that you're eager to come home forever.

I'm excited about that too.

Merry Christmas.

Love,
God

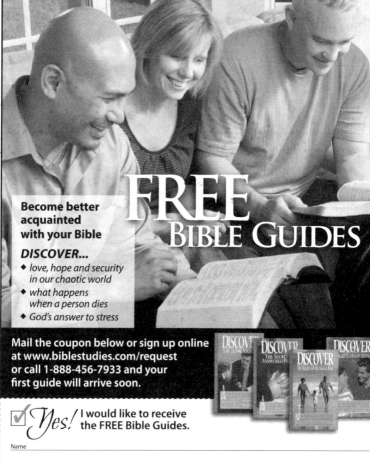